Rude Awakening

RASHANTE PORTER

ISBN 978-1-0980-5622-3 (paperback)
ISBN 978-1-0980-5623-0 (digital)

Christian Faith Publishing, Inc.
832 Park Avenue
Meadville, PA 16335
www.christianfaithpublishing.com

Printed in the United States of America

Acknowledgment

$\mathcal{I}$ would like to thank God who is the head of my life. I would like to thank my husband, Charles Brooks, who helped me accomplish many goals in life, for seeing in me what I couldn't see in myself. I would like to thank my three children—DiOndra Porter, my oldest; Justin Figueroa, my middle and only son; and Genesis Porter my baby. Without the unconditional love of these three, I don't know where I would be. I would like to honor my mom, Grace Nelson, and my dad, Thomas H. Nelson Jr., who encouraged me when I wanted to give up and who thought it not robbery to pray for me. They encouraged me and loved me even when I was unlovable.

I would like to thank my team of women who gather ever Sunday for fellowship and praise: Jacqueline Dawson, Chandra Frazier, Tamika Love, and Shonette Taylor. All of those whom I have named have been my prayer warriors, my encouragement, and my inspiration in writing this book. There are so many others that were there to build me up and pray on my behalf, and I am grateful and truly blessed to have such people in my life. You know who you are. Thank you for the love, patience, and kindness you have shown toward me every day. I love you and I truly thank you.

Introduction

*A*s you read this book, I pray that you will be enlightened, encouraged, and equipped. I pray that wherever you find yourself at in this moment, you will know without a doubt that God is able. Not only is He able to pull you through, bring you out, and strengthen you, but He is also able to meet you right where you are. Surrender your will to God's will and watch how your life will begin to change.

Thank you for taking a time-out to allow me to be an encouragement, an inspiration, and a vessel used for you today. God bless and be encouraged.

A Mother's Love

I look at you and I see a prayer warrior, a woman of strength. I see you bent over on your knees, praying for me and others. When I look at you, Mother, I see a woman of God not afraid to share her wisdom with others—I see my mother. I have not always been in a place where I could appreciate you or, better yet, say thank you for being my mother. You prayed for me through my times of struggles. You held on when I let sin take full control. You spoke words of hope into my soul. You were bold in your belief. You never came up short or tried to pull me down when I was already low, but you did give me hard blows with the Word of God. You gave me the strength I needed for my next hour of trying to get it right. Yes, you gave me the power I needed to take a stand and fight for my life.

You are my mother, my friend, my everything, and I thank God for bringing me into this world through you. I don't know where I would be if it were not for your prayers that pulled me through. You are my mother. Happy mother's day to you. I'm here today, I'm still alive, because your prayers were heard and I survived. I'm still standing and I'm still in touch because I know the prayers of the righteous availeth much. Happy mother's day.

A Marriage So Divine

*W*oven together, molded by the master, a mystery still unknown. Knitted perfectly from the beginning, a masters' love. Hand in hand, a heart that matches in beats, a precious moment that you and I must keep. On each other's finger, we will place a ring. You have found a wife and you have found a good thing. Words softly spoken by the bride and the groom, today is the day we both say, "I do."

Cold feet for sure in both of our shoes. Warm days ahead, I'm so in love with you. All emotions together perfectly intertwined, giving every blessing to a marriage so divine. Touched day by day and hour after hour, strength will be your daily prayer. Oh yes, God will give you power! It was predestined for the two of you to be one heart, one mind, one soul fitted to a tee. A match made, two souls saved, the angels are rejoicing. And our Father, Jehovah God, is smiling at your choices.

One Night with the King

Many times I sit here thinking of that night, that one night I spent with you. You were the perfect man; you took me by the hand and we danced. I gazed into the light, which was so bright; it showed all the rays of color. You were like no other.

So I decided to stay for a while. I decided to get to know you. I wanted to know who you were. What made you smile? What made you cry? Why would I try to stay in your presence? I mean, after all, this was not a dream, or was it a dream? Was it some sort of reality that I was in the presence of a king, a ruler, a redeemer, a healer and not a crook, not a criminal, not a thug, nor a drug dealer? But I was in the presence of God.

I had so much that I wanted to say, to do, so much to show You and I forgot it all. I thought, *Wow, I could have spent the night with a lover, a sister, a brother…a night with a bottle, a needle, a pipe…a night with gossip, with cheating, with stealing.*

I could have spent the night with hanging out and chilling, but I chose to spend the night with You.

I chose to spend the night with the King, the alpha and omega. I chose to spend the night with my beginning and my end. I chose to spend the night with the center of my joy, the real McCoy, the son of the living God. I chose to spend the night with the lily of the valley, the waymaker, the captain of my ship. I chose to spend the night with the one who can lift me up when I am down, the one who can place my feet on solid ground. I chose to spend the night with You.

Jesus, Jesus, Jesus, I wanted to tell You how I felt. I wanted to tell You about my problems. I wanted to tell You how much I love You, but You already knew. So all I could do was bow down and worship as I spent the night with You.

Don't Give Up on You

*F*ollow your dreams, your heart's desires. Let no one tell you you cannot go far. Whatever God called you to do will come natural for you. Much is required, but little energy will do. Don't give up on childhood dreams, don't get caught up in trying to please those who have no vision at all because their vision becomes your vision and you will fall.

Be true to who you are—yes, be true to yourself. Follow every dream and you will have wealth. Keep your mind on the Master who drew out your plan. Put your dream in God's hand and watch it expand. Don't settle for anything but be all you can be because your life is an example for others to see.

Live your life, live for God, and just be your best. Read the Word, get instruction, and He'll do the rest. Dream again, dream big, and don't let your dreams die 'cause the life that you live will be the life of a lie. Be true to who you are—yes, be honest and true.

No one else should be able to steal your dreams. They should teach and encourage you to live out your dreams. God has called us all out of darkness to the light. So your dreams were first visions and you pulled them to sight for others to see your dreams come to pass. Yes! Your dream was put to action and became a thing of the past.

Be careful to think that you did it alone. Give God the glory for that dream He had sown. He planted it in you from the beginning of birth, and then you carried it in your belly until the time to give birth. The pains from that dream you can still feel today. Thank you, God, for the dream, vision, and birth that were created your way.

Be Ye Transformed

*A*re we being transformed? Or have we become conformed to tradition? Are we trusting God and allowing Him to fulfill His purpose? Or are we doing things the way we know how? You see, when you are transformed, you become transparent. You then allow the Holy Spirit to have His way. You no longer have a say in how things will play out because you've taken a back seat and allowed yourself to be able to receive instruction and direction from the Holy Spirit, who is God.

This church has been standing for sixty-seven years, and it's all due to the glory of the master who created the master plan, the master who laid the foundation, the master who used man to fulfill His purpose and His will, the master who is still at work today. You see, we get caught up in the way church used to be run, and we can't see the hand of God in how the church is now being run—different man, same God—and that is why this church is still standing.

It has nothing to do with what we think or how we feel; it has everything to do with being obedient and keeping it real. It has everything to do with putting God first and your thoughts and opinions last. It's about letting God know that we are thirsty for His presence, that we are thirsty for the stirring up of the Holy Spirit, that we are thirsty for the anointing, and also respecting the one God has appointed and anointed to rule over this building, this flock of sheep, to keep us from stumbling and falling asleep.

You see, it's nothing none of us have done, but it's everything God did, everything God is doing, and everything God is going to do. We need to be on one accord. We cannot afford to down one another. We cannot begin to think we've arrived. We still need to strive to become more like Christ. We need to be grateful for the sixty-seven years. We need to be grateful for the pastors who have served and who are now serving. We need to thank God for allowing want to build upon this rock in the last sixty-seven years. We need to look at the sweat and the tears that were and still are flowing through these four walls.

Today, on this sixty-seventh anniversary of Solid Rock Baptist Church, get out of self and get back to God—the founder, the builder, and the provider. It's not about us but it's about Jesus. Don't lose your soul trying to gain the world, but save a soul and cover a multitude of sins. God is still on the throne. Let Him rule and let us serve.

Rewind

The second wind blows your spirit into my soul. Lord, make me whole. Daddy, make me bold for your kingdom. Remove the chains and give me freedom. The second wind blows real deep so my spirit man won't sleep. Awake, arise, and let us get a fresh start. Holy Spirit, do your part. Jesus is our foundation. Now mind, body, and soul rule a nation.

Wait! First, we must gain some patience. Rewind. The second wind begins to share knowledge, wisdom, and understanding. The second wind blows. Push, run, go. Don't slow down for anyone. Your second wind has now begun. Do all you can with what you have this time. The chains are removed, and so is the crime. The blood that was shed was for all. Now rewind. The second wind blows.

No More

No more will I allow you to come into my life and cause disruption. No more will I allow you to creep in. No more will I give you room or space within my inward parts. Knowing that my soul belongs to God, no more will I give an ear to your drama. No more looking back on the past. No more do you get to shape my emotions. I'm kicking you out of this building. No more do you get to separate my family and my friends. No more, Satan; you lose, I win.

No more do you get to confuse our children. I say no more, no more, no more. You don't win. No more suicide, no more drugs being sold, no more babies having babies, no more, not maybe. No more accusing us before God, no more coming in trying to rob, no more stealing or killing.

I plead the blood of Jesus and I say no more. I cover our young girls and boys. I cover our hearts and minds. I cover the front, side, and behind. I cover the mothers and fathers. I cover my family in Christ. I cover the elders and deacons. I cover the ushers, that's right. I cover the choirs and their voices. I cover those on instruments. I plead the blood of Jesus and I cover the pulpit. Get your hands back, move your demonic spirits away.

We lift our hands to God and we begin to share, to share in the same thoughts, to share in total praise, to share in calling on Jesus, and oh yes, our hands we raise. Get thee behind me, Satan, 'cause you are a thing of the past. Your life was for a moment, and oh, you've done your last, your last in causing havoc, your last in causing pain, because we allow Jesus to come into this place. We ask His spirit to dwell. We say, "Lord God, have your way. We won't interrupt your move, Lord God. We need you today. Forgive us for all our wrong,

Lord. Help us to see what You see. And, Father, please help us grow to be all you will have us to be."

No more, no more, no more. You should have killed me when you had the chance. No more because now, I, Rashante Janell Porter, stand.

How Much Can You Gain
if You Lose It All?

*I*n my life, I have lost many things! How much did I gain? In my life, I have gained many things! How much did I lose? See, when you think about it, you've only gained. While entering this world, you had nothing to bring. You've gained a body, a life, and you have good health. We came here poor, but Jesus gave us wealth.

He died and rose and intercedes for us all. We didn't hang from the cross or even take it all. We've gained and we have not been faithful or true. Jesus didn't only die for me, but he died for you too.

We don't even own the clothes on our backs. God provided all so we don't lack. The Bible says every good gift comes from above, not for the good that we have done but because of God's love. He loves us no matter how bad we have sinned. Jesus Christ paid the price so every battle we win.

You can do good all your life and have many things. Give your life back to Christ, be renewed, and be changed. Stop holding on to what doesn't belong to you. Be obedient and do what God has called you to do. I hear the Lord speaking. I will answer His call. How much did you gain if you gambled and lost it all?

Allowing People to Choose

Why do we allow people to choose us when we have already been chosen? Why do we downplay our hurt inside? Why do we try to hide our feelings? You see, we have become so used to putting on a front in front of others. We make ourselves higher than our sister or brother. But deep inside, we're broken, we're confused, we're lost. We get to this place of God where, okay, we put church first but still act our worse by seeing others who are less fortunate pass by. We won't even say hi or let them inside. We act as though this is only a place for us, the so-called believers, or should I say deceivers. What looks good on the outside may be rotten to the core.

Order in the church, and I mean order right now. It's time to bow to the one and only God and stop bowing to self. You are destroying souls and messing with people's health. We were not always saved. We were and still are a mess. The only difference between us and them is, we cover up in our Sunday best. We shine our shoes and put on a nice suit or a cute dress and a hat, if you please. But on the inside, we are covered with a bad heart disease called hatred, envy, jealousy, and lust. Our mouths are filthy, and some of us even cuss. We will tell you all about yourself from Monday to Saturday. Then we sit in church on Sunday, asking God to have us His way.

Get in order, get right, get your life right with God. Open your heart, tell your story, tell of the goodness of God. Go back and remember when your life was a shame. You were not always saved. Give God the glory for all that you do, for He is God alone and He called me and you to be servants. So serve all His people, not just the ones who fit you. You are a servant, and God is the master.

Happy Birthday, I'm Proud of You

I watched as you've grown, how you prayed, how you stayed in God's presence, how you allowed Jehovah to bring you through, raising five children, being abused, being molested, beaten, and mistreated by people who were supposed to watch over and care for you. But in the end, you were still there but were not aware of the pain they had imparted. But thank God for you not turning coldhearted and still being able to bear, still being able to carry not one but five beautiful children whom you've protected, watched over, prayed over, stayed over until they had a turnover.

You are that virtuous woman that Proverbs talks about. You are a mighty woman of God. You are worth bragging about. You're worth more than silver and gold. You are like a pearl or a stone, a rock, a solid ground, not shaking, not moving, but continuously standing still, knowing how to speak and also listen.

I'm proud of you, Mommy, Mother, friend, mentor, God's anointed. I love you with all of my being. I didn't know how to love you before, but I'm very grateful for you. I love everything about you, everything you stand for. When you speak, I hear you, even when we're not in the same room. Your voice is a sweet sound.

I am proud of you and I love you. Happy birthday, Mommy.

Stay True to Yourself

*I*n moments of uncertainty, remember who you are and stay true to self. When problems seem to weigh you down and you feel there's no way out and you feel lost and alone, remember God cares. He hears your prayers. He has already answered you, but you cannot hear what your heart is speaking because you are too busy seeking for the answer. When you are true to you, you know how to be true to others. You'll remove the cover that hid many lies, the makeup that hid the marks of tears that stained your face. When you are true to self, you'll find forgiveness in your heart, you'll take part in saying I was wrong. When you're true to self, you won't stab your brother in the back or see him lack anything. You don't care if you're the leader or the follower; you just want to learn.

God has imparted all we will need for this visit here on earth. All we need to do is push and give birth to what already belongs to us. See, when you're true to self, you don't look for people's praise but you're able to raise one up. When you know who you are, you won't try to figure others out; you'll pray them through.

No matter the situation, when you know who you are, you live for God and not for self. You don't have to look for wealth because it looks for you. When we learn who we are, we can become better not just for self but also for others. We can teach our sisters and brothers right from wrong. Until we learn who we are, we will still go through storm after storm, coming out the same way, not being changed. When we know who we are, we will be able to claim what Jesus proclaimed as ours—victory. When we know who we are, we can be true to ourselves, no more identity crisis. Stay true to yourself.

Rude Awakening

$\mathcal{T}$aken to this dark and lonely place where I can't sleep so I stay awake. Seeking my way back into daylight, closing my eyes and holding my breath tight. Then I realized I was mistaken, only to know I had a rude awakening.

Shaken, beaten, stabbed, even shot—yeah, that was the punishment I got. So I kneeled down on both my knees and asked the Lord to help me. "Please take me from this place I was taken."

He said, "Baby girl, this is a rude awakening. I had to show you where you would end up if you don't drink from your bitter cup."

So I said, "Lord, have mercy on me and give me your light so that I can see."

He said, "First, you must endure some pain but trust in God and call on Jesus's name."

I said, "Lord, I've tried but I don't know how to pray. Let me touch the hem of your garment, and I will be okay."

He said, "Keep hope, keep trust, keep faith in the end and be blessed and experience a spiritual awakening."

Trapped in My Mind

As I begin to apply the Word of God to every negative thought, I am released in my way of thinking. I am renewed in my mind, no longer defined by words people spoke, no longer defined by what I believe, but now I received the truth, which is the Word of God. I was lost in my thinking, in my thoughts, in my deed, and I didn't believe what I thought I believed. I was confused, confined, locked up, a prisoner in my own mind. I didn't know how I got there but I knew I had to seek, to call out for help, but I didn't know how, so I cried inwardly so no one could hear. I covered up my thoughts by being careful of what I said only to realize my speaking lined up with my thoughts. "I need help," I said.

I need help so I can't begin to call out outwardly, but no one answered. Everyone was deaf to my cry, blind to my actions because they were the same, but then I encountered a worshipper, a prayer warrior, a God-pleaser, not a people-pleaser, and she began to give me what I needed. She gave me tough love, tough words, but all in love. She was real. She loved me so much. She broke me down and built me up at the same time. I never experienced this type of love, so I didn't understand what was going on.

Everything she was I wanted to be, and all she wanted to do was to love and be a blessing to me, but I couldn't see that until one day she decided to back away. I could not stay away from her. It was something I needed and something she wanted, and that was love. I'm no longer trapped, and she's no longer stuck because this day both our minds have been renewed in Christ. We are not just married in spirit, but now we're married in truth. No longer trapped in my mind, we have been set free together.

Brought with a Price

*Y*ou and I were bought with a price. We are not being rented with the option to buy, so why are we living like the leased-out property? UC we were purchased with the blood of Christ. We were bought with pure love. We were conceived out of His death and then we grew into His resurrection. We are not being rented, we are not being borrowed. We have life today and eternal life tomorrow. We can never be sold back because the blood paid for it all. It paid for the sin in the garden; it paid for men's fall.

Stop renting out your mind to the thoughts of negative. Stop renting out your mouth like one who doesn't know how to live. Stop renting out your hands to touch the dirty things. Stop renting out your feet to walk on anything. Stop living as one who thinks you paid the price for your blood was tainted and Jesus's blood was right. He bought your whole being, your body, mind, and soul. He set you free from sin by dying and being bold. He didn't have to do it but He loved us just that much.

Don't live your life renting because you own so much. Stop renting and start owning. Jesus paid the debt for you and me.

Pleasing You and Losing Me

*T*oo busy trying to please you, I missed out on all lights offers. Having you being a tease to me, I fell for the underlined nonsense, never really expressing how I feel because I know I will keep it real. I hate living behind a fast tongue and a slow mind. Never been able to define who I am.

You brought to the table a recipe I never heard of, never tasted or touched. I thought you brought a little too much of that appetizer called love. You see, I wasn't looking for a taste test or a sample. I was looking for a full-course meal, a side order of communication, a portion of wisdom, a taste of understanding. I wasn't being demanding. I was just hungry, hungry for a dinner called love.

Instead, you gave me half of that; you gave me a side order of silence, a portion of bitterness. You even tried to serve me selfishness. But desert, who would have thought I was eating a dish called anger, miscommunication, and loneliness?

Wow, now I'm back at your restaurant again, put it in another order. I thought maybe things would change. I mean, you did rearrange your thoughts and your plans. I thought, *Oops, there goes my skirt right over my head, oh my.*

That's how I feel when I'm around you. I feel as though you have a split personality, one being formal and one being a fugitive. You never give all of you; it's like you're fleeing from trying to live in this place that has been a blessing for you.

Today is the day for you to choose. Who will you serve, God or man? You cannot serve both; you will love one and hate the other. It's time to choose. Choose Christ, my brother.

Granted

I went down to the courthouse today and I pressed charges against the devil. Upon entering the courthouse, I saw others from the body of Christ also entering. I asked them what they were here for, and they replied, "You are going to need support, right?"

While thanking them for their support, I looked away and saw the pastor, and he approached me. I asked him if he had come to be supportive too. He answered, "I have come as a witness. I have seen what the devil tried to do."

Then while I was talking to him, I heard the choir singing. Upon entering the court, I asked what they were doing here. They replied, "We are the juror and we will sing about the case."

When I began to enter the court, I was ushered in by the Holy Spirit. I looked at the other side where the defendant should be sitting, but no one was there. I looked at the seat where the judge sits, and no one was there. I began to hear within my body the Holy Spirit speak and say, "Present your case."

I started by saying, "Good morning, Your Honor." I then carried on with the charges. I said, "Your Honor, for the past thirty-nine years of my life, this serpent has been able to throw me offtrack. He has tried to attack my body with sickness. He tried to get me to become angry. He even tried to steal my children." I went on to say, "Your Honor, I didn't come here to place a restraining order against him. I came that I may seek the death penalty." I then said, "Allow me to crush his head by keeping him under my feet so that he may rise no more."

"Your request has been granted."

For This, We Call You Pastor

You are a humble man, a gentleman, a man after God's own heart. You were set apart for times such as these, not to please man but to please God. And for this, we call you pastor. You were called out of your father's body and into your mother's womb. You were then called for to preach—to preach Jesus, to preach the truth, to stir up the spirit. You were sent as proof that Jesus lives because He lives in you, and for this we call you pastor.

You are a man of many hats, for you wear the hat of a God-fearing man, the hat of the child of God, the hat of a family man, a pastor, a provider, and a friend; but when it comes to doing the will of God, there is no end. You go back for your sheep and you try to keep them at peace with one another. You know each one of us by name, and for this, we proclaim and call you pastor.

Five years of God's grace and favor, five years of preaching and teaching with love, five years of faithful service to the one who sits above. Five years of leading by example, five years is just a sample of what God has for you. Pastor, you are not through—oh, you're just getting started. The fire is just starting to burn, you are still in the place of learning on heavenly things above. That's why God allowed your rib to be put back at your side, so He can lift you up when you slip and slide, so He can feel you up when you pour out to us because He had to give you someone you can trust. And for this, we call you pastor.

You are not only a leader in the church but also a leader in your home. Although I don't live there, I can see it through your family. You are the true meaning of Joshua 24:15, which says, "But as for me and my house we will serve the Lord."

Not only do you have wisdom but you also have love, and we know that love is what God sees when he looks at you. Thank you for not just being a pastor but for also being true. For this, I call you a servant, a friend, a man of God, but most of all, I call you blessed. And for this, we call you pastor.

The Inside Cry

I cry on the inside because they are no longer flowing where they are shown. I cried deeply for the pain I feel when no one around seems to keep it real. I cry for those who cannot cry for themselves, oh, and for those who cannot see another way. I cry for the people who have no roof over their heads or, better yet, have not been fed. I cry for the boy who tries to become a man without a man lending a helping hand. I cry for the child who is born with birth defects, not knowing God can correct them. I cry for those who are lost in their soul, body, and mind, not realizing they have been blind. I'll cry for the little girl who's giving birth all because she decided to lift her skirt. I cried for the cold hearts I felt around me because of a melt-down they could not see. I cry for the man who was crucified, but my tears turned to joy when he was resurrected. Because He lives, I live.

To Forgive Means to Let It Go

Sometimes we feel as though we have to hold on to things. Like, we must continuously remind ourselves of the past—past mistakes, past failures, and past relationships. We act as though we must hold on to the thing or things that hurt the most.

How can we begin a fresh start if we're constantly bringing up our past or allowing someone else to bring up our past? If you find yourself stuck in your past, whether it's through you or anyone else, it's time to break free. It's time to really be set free from your past.

When God told Lot's wife not to look back or she would be turned into a pillar of salt, she looked back. Not only that, she was leaving behind what God had told Lot to leave behind. When God tells you to let go and not look behind, that's what He means. He does not mean go and turn around in your mind. He needs your actions and thoughts to be on one accord.

My prayer today is, "Father God, my Lord and my savior, please help me to become more like You. Help me to be more obedient and less concerned about what or who I may be leaving behind. Help me to hear You even through distractions. Help me to make You my number one priority. Allow me to even put You before me. Lord God, even when I come so often, I pray that I will begin to hear You whisper in my ear and pull me back. Help me, Father. I pray that where I am weak, Lord God, You make me strong. I pray that where there is sickness, Lord God, You make me whole. I pray that You, Lord God, be the shelter for every storm in my life. Help me to put behind every failure, every mistake, and every ungodly word that I have made or spoken and allow me to think before I act or speak. Father God, keep me out of harm's way. Let me not be so quick to become angry but help me to be quick to put the fire out. For I know that my tongue may become few sometimes, Father God, I ask that You make it a water hose to put out every flame that I may encounter. Keep me from turning back and allow me to stay on a forward path. Let your will be done, Lord God, in Jesus's mighty name. Amen. And so be it."

Don't turn around, don't look back.

Giving You the Best of Me

I give myself away so You can use me, Lord. I no longer try to do it by myself. I release and I ask for your help. I pull back my hands out of that situation. I place it in your hands and watch You erase it or replace it with your will. I give myself away to You, Lord God, meaning I hand over my burdens, my plans, my emotions, and I'm ready to be demoted so that You can be promoted and I may go higher. And You search me, dear God, and clean out oil residue that has tried to hide itself from you. Yes, clean the residue so that you can reside in places like my heart, my mind, and my soul, dear Lord. Make Me bold not for myself but for You.

I give over my hands so that You can use them for healing. I give over my mouth so that it will bless You. I give over my feet so that I will be able to walk the streets with truth. I give over my eyes to You, Lord God, so that I can see the love of You even and others that are bound and in those who have no truth. I give over my lips, oh Lord, that they should not be so fast to speak. Heal my tongue, my lips, and my eyes, Lord. Give me the wisdom of You.

I want to be eager to do your will, not the will of self or man. My prayer for today is that you lead and guide me, Lord. Please take my hand.

You see, we may think we are pleasing You, Father God, by showing up early Sunday morning while the rest of the week we are just getting by and can't figure out what we're doing. So here I stand, asking for You to send the angels out before me and make me fall down to my knees every day and give You all the glory. Let my worship be real for You.

I have so much that I want to say, so much that needs to be done. In so many battles I've tried to fight, those battles You've already won. Keep me from becoming bitter. Keep anger away from my path. Lead me on a journey for You because that's the only walk that will last. Give me the living water that you promised in your Word, dress me in your armor, wash me in your blood, cover me with the love of Christ, and keep me at your feet. Let my mind think your thoughts, Lord. Let my spirit speak.

You said while we are on this journey, You will lead us all the way through. You said a wise woman builds a house and a foolish woman tears it down with her hands. Give me the strength to build and never tear down, give me the Master's plan.

Oh, let me listen as the Holy Spirit leads. Let me continue to read your Word. Let me write it on the tablet of my heart so that it will always be heard. Now as we face this day, dear Lord, allow us to give ourselves away to you, heavenly Father. In Jesus's name I pray. Amen.

Warring Hands

Teach my hands to war for You, oh Lord. Teach me how to soar above every issue, every circumstance. Teach me how to stand still and wait on You. Teach me how to rest in You, oh Lord, how to rely on your promises—oh, the rest on your breast when I grow weary. Teach me how to walk in the steps you have ordered. Teach my son and my daughters how to take it one day at a time. Teach me how to pray, oh Lord. Teach me how to stay in your presence. Teach me how to speak life, how to do what is right, how to use my tongue to please You, not being ashamed to bring praise upon your name.

Teach my heart to catch every word You have spoken, not taking anything for granted. Teach me how to love even my enemies when they befriend me only to kill me. Teach me how to praise your name, how to raise my voice, oh Lord, how to shift the atmosphere. Teach me how to listen and not speak, to be slow, to take offense but to defend your every word.

Teach me how to spread the love You have loved me with, the love that covered all my sins. Teach me how to teach the people to war, to cry out, to shout without a doubt knowing You hear us.

Teach me how to go to the throne and fall to my knees so that I may be pleasing to You. Teach me how to war in the spirit where the demons can hear it and fear it. Let it cause an earthquake. Teach me how to war, God. Teach me how to walk, oh God. Teach me how to rest, oh God. Teach me how to lean, oh God, in You.

Christian Women Seeking the Glory of God to Impact a Lost World

*W*hen I think about the goodness of God, I think about the stars, the moon, the sun, and daylight. I begin to seek Him more. Meaning, I begin to go deep and worship deeper and praise deeper in the lifting of my hands and the kneeling at His feet. I begin to want to please God, not self.

When I think about the greatness of God, I think greater is He that is in me than He that is in this world. I begin to think of the sky and the sea, the heaven and the earth, the creation God birthed out of nothing.

I begin to speak more of His glory. When I look at the faces, I see the places I've seen and all that my God has done for me. I worship in His glory because He is the author of my story. See, when we stop looking at others, when we stop trying to be in charge and become a part of the children of God, we can relax in His glory.

You get to trade in those dirty rags for a clean garment. You get to trade in that sickness for healing. You get to trade in your nasty ways and replace it with the love of God. You begin to want more of God and less of self. You begin to lend a hand and be of help. You will not continue to stab your brother in the back. You will not see your children begging or be in lack. You will not talk about your neighbor's issues. You will not try to be the leader but you'll say, "I got you."

When you're seeking more of God's presence, all of your don'ts and wants turn into "My soul says yes." You begin to want the best. You become all God has called you to be. You fall to your knees and begin to plead, asking God to forgive all the wrong you have done, all the things you have said for all the times you went astray.

The Bible tells us that God has called us out of darkness and into His marvelous light, so He allows us to share in His glory, not to take the glory and glorify ourselves. We need to learn to forgive and be forgiven to be still in His presence, to let the glory of God fill out temples, to let His glory be seen in our every situation. And in every storm, to God be the glory; it's God's alone.

He is, oh, He is worthy. He is faithful and just. He is my all in all. Oh, He is my waymaker. He is my joy, my peace, my strength. He is my healer, my deliverer, and my redeemer. He is my rock, my shepherd, and my provider. God is glory. So I will seek more of His glory. I will share in His glory. I will give Him the glory.

Let God's presence illuminate your life. Be grateful for the fact that God dwells in you, that He is for you, and no one can be against you. Ask God to enlarge your territory so that you may be able to praise Him more and find peace in His presence.

My Place of Destiny

*A*s I walked down the aisles to my place of destiny, I reached you along the path and I received your hand in marriage and I said, "I do." It was planned from the day of my birth that I will be a part of you. God has woven us together, fitted us perfectly, intertwined us in a picture of perfect love. I knew from that very moment that I love you, have loved you, and will always love you.

My reason for being is you. My life of worship I can share with you. Giving you permission to take care of my heart, I put it in your hands and asked you to take good care of it. Knowing now what I didn't know before, you are the door that I am now walking through. You were the prayer that has now been answered.

A question no longer remains because we're no longer two but one of the same. Although we may have some storms along the way, I'm here to stay. And to say with you this day, "I do," oh, I do open my mind, I do open my heart. I give the best of me to you.

To Forgive Means to Let It Go

*S*ometimes we feel as though we have to hold on to things. Like, we must continuously remind ourselves of the past—past mistakes, past failures, and past relationships. We act as though we must hold on to the thing or things that hurt the most.

How can we begin a fresh start if we're constantly bringing up our past or allowing someone else to bring up our past? If you find yourself stuck in your past, whether it's through you or anyone else, it's time to break free. It's time to really be set free from your past.

When God told Lot's wife not to look back or she would be turned into a pillar of salt, she looked back. Not only that, she was leaving behind what God had told Lot to leave behind. When God tells you to let go and not look behind, that's what He means. He does not mean go and turn around in your mind. He needs your actions and thoughts to be on one accord.

My prayer today is, "Father God, my Lord and my savior, please help me to become more like You. Help me to be more obedient and less concerned about what or who I may be leaving behind. Help me to hear You even through distractions. Help me to make You my number one priority. Allow me to even put You before me. Lord God, even when I come so often, I pray that I will begin to hear You whisper in my ear and pull me back. Help me, Father. I pray that where I am weak, Lord God, You make me strong. I pray that where there is sickness, Lord God, You make me whole. I pray that You, Lord God, be the shelter for every storm in my life. Help me to put behind every failure, every mistake, and every ungodly word that I have made or spoken and allow me to think before I act or speak. Father God, keep me out of harm's way. Let me not be so quick to become angry but help me to be quick to put the fire out. For I know that my tongue

36

may become few sometimes, Father God, I ask that You make it a water hose to put out every flame that I may encounter. Keep me from turning back and allow me to stay on a forward path. Let your will be done, Lord God, in Jesus's mighty name. Amen. And so be it."

Don't turn around, don't look back.

Giving You the Best of Me

I give myself away so You can use me, Lord. I no longer try to do it by myself. I release and I ask for your help. I pull back my hands out of that situation. I place it in your hands and watch You erase it or replace it with your will. I give myself away to You, Lord God, meaning I hand over my burdens, my plans, my emotions, and I'm ready to be demoted so that You can be promoted and I may go higher. And You search me, dear God, and clean out oil residue that has tried to hide itself from you. Yes, clean the residue so that you can reside in places like my heart, my mind, and my soul, dear Lord. Make Me bold not for myself but for You.

I give over my hands so that You can use them for healing. I give over my mouth so that it will bless You. I give over my feet so that I will be able to walk the streets with truth. I give over my eyes to You, Lord God, so that I can see the love of You even and others that are bound and in those who have no truth. I give over my lips, oh Lord, that they should not be so fast to speak. Heal my tongue, my lips, and my eyes, Lord. Give me the wisdom of You.

I want to be eager to do your will, not the will of self or man. My prayer for today is that you lead and guide me, Lord. Please take my hand.

You see, we may think we are pleasing You, Father God, by showing up early Sunday morning while the rest of the week we are just getting by and can't figure out what we're doing. So here I stand, asking for You to send the angels out before me and make me fall down to my knees every day and give You all the glory. Let my worship be real for You.

I have so much that I want to say, so much that needs to be done. In so many battles I've tried to fight, those battles You've already won. Keep me from becoming bitter. Keep anger away from my path. Lead me on a journey for You because that's the only walk that will last. Give me the living water that you promised in your Word, dress me in your armor, wash me in your blood, cover me with the love of Christ, and keep me at your feet. Let my mind think your thoughts, Lord. Let my spirit speak.

You said while we are on this journey, You will lead us all the way through. You said a wise woman builds a house and a foolish woman tears it down with her hands. Give me the strength to build and never tear down, give me the Master's plan.

Oh, let me listen as the Holy Spirit leads. Let me continue to read your Word. Let me write it on the tablet of my heart so that it will always be heard. Now as we face this day, dear Lord, allow us to give ourselves away to you, heavenly Father. In Jesus's name I pray. Amen.

The Inside Cry

I cry on the inside because they are no longer flowing where they are shown. I cried deeply for the pain I feel when no one around seems to keep it real. I cry for those who cannot cry for themselves, oh, and for those who cannot see another way. I cry for the people who have no roof over their heads or, better yet, have not been fed. I cry for the boy who tries to become a man without a man lending a helping hand. I cry for the child who is born with birth defects, not knowing God can correct them. I cry for those who are lost in their soul, body, and mind, not realizing they have been blind. I'll cry for the little girl who's giving birth all because she decided to lift her skirt. I cried for the cold hearts I felt around me because of a meltdown they could not see. I cry for the man who was crucified, but my tears turned to joy when he was resurrected. Because He lives, I live.

About the Author

My name is Rashante Porter. I am a child of God, a forty-seven-year old mother of three. I was born and raised in Passaic, New Jersey, before moving to Paterson, New Jersey, sixteen years ago. I'm a security guard for Motivated Security here in Paterson, New Jersey.

I started writing poetry at a very young age. It was my way of expressing my true feelings, by writing them down on paper. I did not recognize my gift of writing until I started reading my poetry in front of a church full of Christians. It was there I received criticism and praise. I say criticism and praise because some would be offended by my work and some would consider change because of what they heard. I am very grateful that God has chosen me to not only write but also speak His Word through poetry.

CPSIA information can be obtained
at www.ICGtesting.com
Printed in the USA
LVHW091112031120
670569LV00004B/612

9 781098 056223